BIG BOOK OF
TRAINS

National Railway Museum, York

DORLING KINDERSLEY
London • New York • Moscow • Sydney

A Dorling Kindersley Book

Editor Jane Yorke
Designer Veneta Altham
Senior Managing Editor Sarah Phillips
Senior Managing Art Editor Peter Bailey

DTP Designer Greg Bryant
Production Josie Alabaster
Jacket Design Andrew Nash
Picture Research James T. Robinson,
Christine Rista

Photography Mike Dunning,
Richard Leeney
National Railway Museum Consultants
Christine Heap, Stephen Hoadley, David Mosley
National Railway Museum web address: http//www.nmsi.ac.uk/nrm/

Published in Great Britain by
Dorling Kindersley Limited
9 Henrietta Street
London WC2E 8PS

2 4 6 8 10 9 7 5 3 1

Visit us on the World Wide Web at
http://www.dk.com

A CIP catalogue record for this book is available
from the British Library.

ISBN: 0-7513-5850-9

Colour reproduction by Flying Colours, Italy
Printed and bound in Italy by Mondadori

Dorling Kindersley would like to thank *Le Shuttle*,
Calais, France for its help with photography.

The publisher would like to thank the following for their kind
permission to reproduce their photographs:

a = above; c = centre; b = below/bottom; l = left;
r = right; t = top.

Alvey & Towers: 2 ca, 3 tl, tr, 6 cl, 6-7, 8 tl, 12 tl, 25 tr, 26 c, 28;
Central Japan Railway Company: 23 tr; **Colour-rail:** 2 b, 10-11;
Sylvia Cordaiy Photo Library: Geoffrey Taunton 31 tl; **Greater
North Eastern Railways:** Fastline Photographic 24 bl; **Robert
Harding Picture Library:** Bildagentur Schuster/Gluske 15 tr;
I. Griffiths 3 cbr, 29 tr; M. Short 29 b; **Images Colour Library:** 12-13;
Impact Photos: Philip Gordon 23 br; **Brian Jennison:** 30 bl, 31 tr;
Anthony J. Lambert: 3 car, 14 tl, 27; **Richard Leeney:** 19 tr;
Milepost 92½: 19 br; Brian Lovell 3 bl, 22-23; **National Railway
Museum, York:** 4 c; **NPS Photo:** Ken Ganz 10 tl; **Photo Affairs
Bildarchiv:** Jürgen Bögelspacher 3 cbl, 20 tr, 20-21, 21 tr, 26 b, 29 tl;
QA Photos: 3 cl, 16 bl, 18-19; **Quadrant Picture Library:** Railway
Gazette 21 cr; **Science Museum:** 2 t, 4 bl, 4-5, 7 tr; **South American
Pictures:** Tony Morrison 26 t; **Spectrum Colour Library:** D. & J.
Heaton 22 tr; **Swedish State Railways:** Industrifotografen AB 24-25;
Telegraph Colour Library: Bildagentur 24 cl; **Jim Winkley:** 3 cal,
br, 9 tl, tr, 12 bl, 14-15, 30-31; Mike Bledsoe 11 t.

Jacket: **Images Colour Library:** front; **Milepost 92½:** Brian Soloman
back tr, spine b; **QA Photos:** back b; **Telegraph Colour Library:**
Japack Photo Library spine a.

Early steam locomotives   4

American steam locomotives   6

Fast steam locomotives   8

Powerful steam locomotives   10

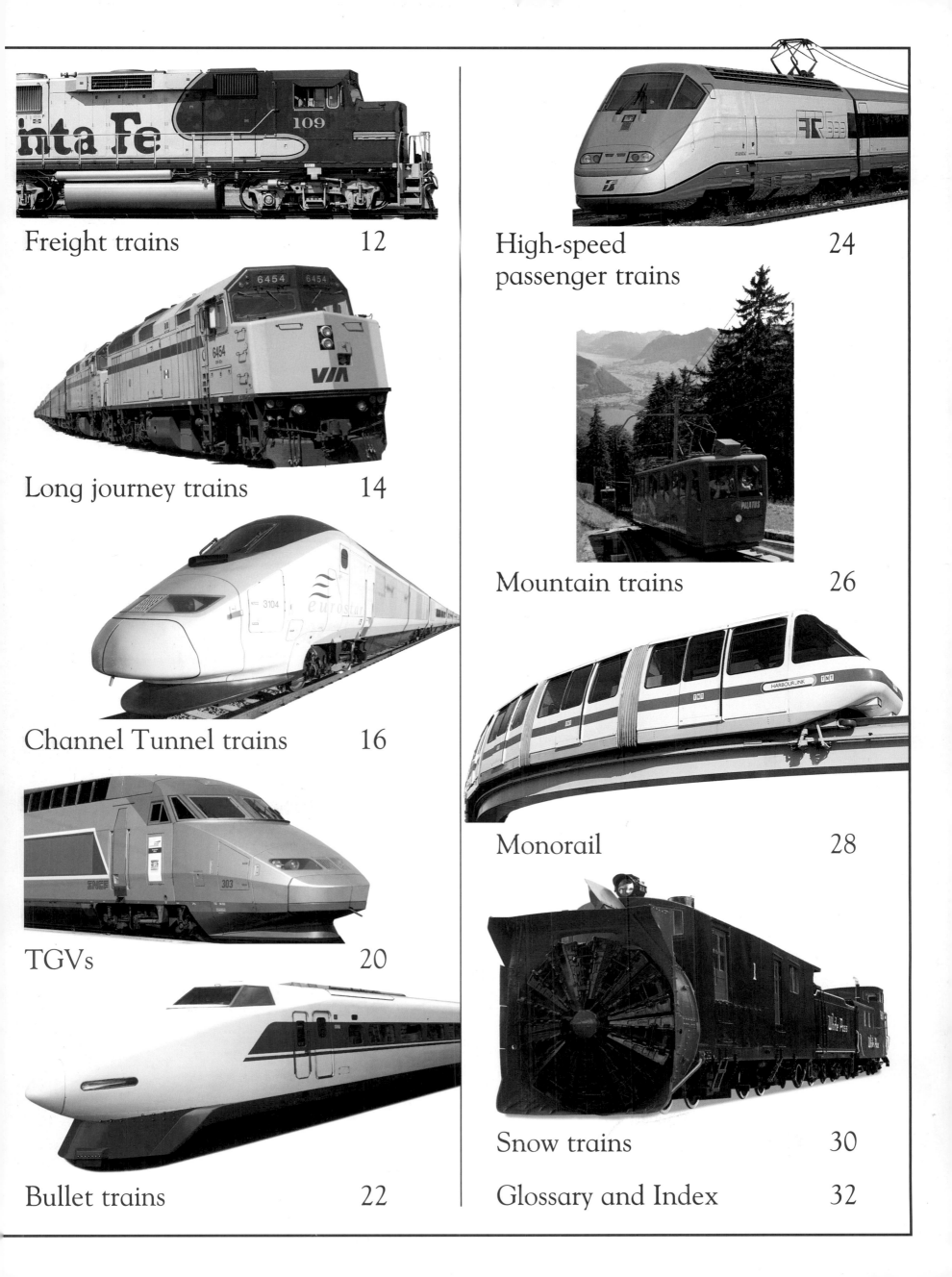

Freight trains 12

Long journey trains 14

Channel Tunnel trains 16

TGVs 20

Bullet trains 22

High-speed passenger trains 24

Mountain trains 26

Monorail 28

Snow trains 30

Glossary and Index 32

Early steam locomotives

In Britain, the first railways were built to carry coal, and horses were used to pull the trucks along. In 1804, Richard Trevithick built the first steam locomotive, but it was slower than a horse and so heavy that it kept breaking the track. Soon people were making reliable steam locomotives that could carry goods and passengers quickly over longer distances.

This cut-away replica of Rocket *enables you to see inside the boiler*

The tender carried coke for fuel. Water was carried in the barrel

First-class passenger carriages were similar to stage coaches

First railway

Rocket worked on the Liverpool and Manchester Railway, opened in 1830. This was the first railway to provide passenger trains pulled by steam locomotives.

Rocket locomotive

Rocket was designed by Robert Stephenson in 1829. This 4.5-tonne steam locomotive was successful because the design used all the latest ideas. It could travel at speeds of up to 40 kilometres per hour on its intercity journey.

Exhaust steam went up the tall chimney

The boiler heated water to make steam

The steam pushed the pistons and the connecting rods turned the wheels

The fireman shovelled coke into the firebox. The heat from the fire passed along tubes inside the boiler

The driver and fireman stood on a small platform

The huge cylinders containing the pistons were upright on this engine

Puffing Billy *took its name from the loud noise made by the exhaust steam*

Transporting coal

Puffing Billy is one of the oldest surviving steam locomotives. It was built in England in 1813, to a design by William Hedley. The locomotive worked for 48 years on a railway just eight kilometres long. It pulled wagons of coal at walking pace from Wylam colliery to a nearby river for transportation by barge.

The pistons made the beams rock backwards and forwards. These moved the connecting rods, which turned the wheels

The boiler produced steam, which entered the cylinders and pushed the pistons

The tender carried the coke fuel supply

The locomotive ran on cast-iron, "fish-bellied" rails. These had a thicker mid-section for added strength

The connecting rods moved cogs, which turned the wheels

American steam locomotives

Railways soon spread all over the world, carrying people and goods faster than anything else had before. The first railway built across the United States of America was finished in May 1869. Colourful steam locomotives, like the ones shown here, carried settlers travelling to the new towns in the west. These locomotives were called 4-4-0s, because they had four driving wheels and four bogie wheels to guide the engine on the sometimes poor track. The bogie could swivel from side to side around the twisting tracks.

The chimney let out smoke and used steam

A large, powerful oil lamp warned people that a train was coming at night

Door into the smokebox

The cowcatcher was a strong, metal grid, which protected the locomotive from coming off the track if it hit a buffalo on the line

Wood-burning locomotive

Jupiter was an early American locomotive that burned wood for fuel. This famous engine worked on the Central Pacific Railroad. It had a large funnel-shaped chimney to catch the shower of sparks that came out of the engine with the smoke and steam.

Coal-burning locomotive

By 1875, some American steam locomotives were using coal for fuel. This model shows how much of the pipework was on the outside for easy maintenance.

Tender

Warning bell

Four driving wheels

Four-wheeled bogie

Cowcatcher

The sand box sprinkled sand on to wet rails to give the wheels more grip

The boiler turned the water into steam

The steam whistle used to warn people and animals of the train's approach

The firebox burned the coal to heat the water

Heading out west

Locomotive 119 travelled westwards across America on the Union Pacific Railroad. The engine weighed 36 tonnes and could pull about six passenger carriages. At full steam, it could speed along at 80 kilometres per hour.

The large cab protected the driver and fireman from the wind and weather

The tender carried four tonnes of coal and 9,000 litres of water to power the train for 150 kilometres

The steam pushed the piston, which moved the connecting rod and turned the wheels

Fast steam locomotives

Large cylinders make the engine very powerful

The casing opens up for cleaning the inside of the engine

No 4498
CLASS A4

Locomotive engineer

This locomotive is an A4 Class, the same type as *Mallard*. It is named *Sir Nigel Gresley*, after the mechanical engineer who designed the engines.

Some passenger trains, called express trains, are designed to run non-stop between two cities. In the 1930s, the finest steam locomotives ever built pulled such trains. Some had sleek, streamlined shapes to help them go faster, and bigger engines that could run for long periods at speeds of over 160 kilometres per hour.

Fastest steam locomotive

Mallard holds the unbeaten record as the fastest steam locomotive in the world. On 3 July 1938, it reached a speed of 202 kilometres per hour running downhill between Grantham and Peterborough, in England. This speed record was set during the trials of brake equipment on the streamlined coaches of the London and North Eastern Railway.

4468

The driver and fireman operated the locomotive from the footplate

These rods drove a very accurate speedometer

This plaque commemorates Mallard's *record-breaking run in 1938*

The smokebox door can be opened to clean the soot out of the front of the engine

The locomotive number is painted on the front of the engine

Famous express train

Flying Scotsman is one of the most famous locomotives in the world. In 1928, it headed the first non-stop express train from London to Edinburgh, in Scotland, a distance of 665 kilometres. On its daily run in 1934, the train set a speed record for steam locomotives of 161 kilometres per hour.

Train attraction

Flying Scotsman is still kept in working order today, so that passengers can enjoy travelling on a train pulled by this very famous locomotive.

Mallard can be seen on display at the National Railway Museum in York

The specially designed double chimney let out steam and smoke efficiently

The streamlined nose and engine casing helped the locomotive to travel at high speeds

The engine weighed 165 tonnes and was over 21 metres long

Mallard was a 4-6-2 locomotive. It had four leading wheels, six large 2-metre driving wheels, and two trailing wheels

Powerful steam locomotives

By the 1940s, engineers were designing bigger and more powerful steam engines to pull heavy freight trains at higher speeds. These huge locomotives often had two sets of cylinders and driving wheels under one very large boiler. They were called articulated engines because the driving wheels could pivot under the boiler to travel around tight bends.

Big Boy weighed 230 tonnes

Biggest steam locomotive

America's Union Pacific Railroad had 25 *Big Boy* locomotives built between 1941 and 1944, based on Anatole Mallet's idea. These monster engines were 40 metres long, five metres high, and had 16 driving wheels. They could travel at 130 kilometres per hour.

The large boiler supplied steam to the two power units

The bunker and tank held 36,000 litres of water and 25 tonnes of coal

African freight

From 1954, the 20A Class Garratt locomotive hauled loads of coal and copper in the countries now called Zambia and Zimbabwe. This articulated locomotive had engine units at the front and back, with the boiler slung between them. The design enabled the powerful locomotive to travel around bends on light track in the African bush.

The front engine unit had four leading wheels, eight driving wheels, and two trailing wheels

The driver had a poor view down the length of the huge boiler

American giant
The Challenger was the *Big Boy*'s little cousin, being only 37 metres long. The engine had 12 driving wheels and was used to haul passengers and goods trains over the Rocky Mountains and across the western deserts.

This 4-6-6-4 locomotive had six front driving wheels, powered by a set of cylinders

The cowcatcher prevented animals on the track from becoming trapped under the locomotive

The heavy engine could pull 1,400 tonnes of freight

Water for the boiler was carried in this tank at the front of the engine

The brake pipes ran the entire length of the train and enabled the driver to control all of the train vehicles

Freight trains

Today's cleaner, diesel-electric locomotives have replaced the powerful steam locomotives of the past. These modern engines are able to haul large amounts of freight over long distances using less fuel than trucks would need. They transport all sorts of goods: food produce like wheat and eggs, coal for industry, cars, and even tanks!

The locomotive runs at a top speed of 100 kilometres per hour

Long-haul journeys

The Santa Fe diesel-electric locomotive is used to haul freight hundreds of kilometres across the United States of America, from California to Chicago. The large fuel tanks keep the engines going on the long desert runs.

Huge tanks carry up to 1,750 litres of diesel fuel

The driver enters the cab using the steps and a door in the front of the locomotive

The air brakes act directly on the wheels to stop the train safely

Pulling power

This heavy freight train crossing the American deserts of Arizona is hauled by five diesel engines, operated by just one driver. The whole train is almost two kilometres long. Behind the locomotives, there are five double-decker freight cars. The following 80 or more cars carry freight in road-trailers, loaded in a "piggy-back" fashion.

The small snowplough can clear snowdrifts or debris off the line

The driver's cab is fully protected against the weather

Locomotive identification number

Powerful freight locomotive
This freight locomotive of the American Santa Fe Railroad is 15 metres long and weighs 112 tonnes. Diesel oil fuels the engine that generates electricity to drive the wheels.

8270

8270

The 12 driving wheels are powered by electric motors

Long journey trains

Some train journeys take days to complete. The trains are equipped w[ith] everything that the passengers need [to] spend a long time on board. There [are] carriages with seats for use in the d[ay] and sleeping cars with beds where th[e] travellers spend the night. Meals are served in the restaurant car.

Ventilator grills allow air in to cool the diesel engine. The engine drives the electric generator, which powers the electric motors

Observation carriages

The Canadian Pacific Railway attaches special observation carriages with viewing domes at the end of its trains. The upper-level seats enable passengers to get a good view of the spectacular scenery, as they travel through the Rocky Mountains.

The large fuel tanks allow the locomotive to travel long distances before re-fuelling

The train has a luggage car, which also includes living quarters for the train crew

Electric motors turn the locomotive's wheels

Crossing Canada

A journey on the Canadian Trans-continental takes three days from Vancouver to Toronto, a distance of 4,459 kilometres. The train is long and heavy with up to 19 carriages. It is pulled by a large, powerful diesel locomotive running at a top speed of 166 kilometres per hour.

Two locomotives are used for extra hauling power where there are steep gradients

...ain journey

...ays to travel on the Trans-Siberian Express
...o Vladivostok in the Russian Federation.
...9 kilometres long and the train stops at
...g the way. This makes it the longest
...h the world without changing trains.

*...up steps into
...om here, he
...of the*

Insid...

The cab...
complic...
main c...
control...
and rev...
The tro...
which...

...
...

*Powerfu...
of the tr...*

*On some parts of the line,
the Trans-Siberian Express
runs on electricity picked
up from an overhead wire*

*The strong
headlights let
people see the
train coming*

6454   6454

VIA

*The co...
behind...*

*The s...
train...
high-s...*

TGVs

The *Train à Grande Vitesse,* or TGV, is France's high-speed electric train. It came into service in 1981, running on special tracks between Paris to Lyon. In 1990, an improved TGV *Atlantique* linked Paris and Bordeaux. The TGV travels at speeds of up to 300 kilometres per hour.

Locomotives at both ends
All TGVs have a powerful electric motor unit, or engine, attached to the front and back of the train.

The locomotive's eight driving wheels are powered by electric motors

Computer controls

When travelling at top speeds, it takes the TGV nearly 3.5 kilometres to stop safely. The braking systems are controlled by a computer in the driver's cab.

The pantograph picks up electricity from overhead wires

The TGV runs at its fastest on a growing network of special tracks. It can use ordinary tracks but has to run at slower speeds

The streamlined body helps the train to travel at high speeds

Fast ride

Riding in the TGV is very comfortable even at high speeds. Passengers are able to eat a meal, use the telephone, or watch a video on the train.

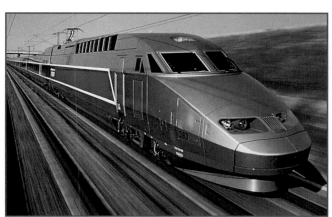

Intercity passenger train

The high-speed, grey-and-blue TGV *Atlantique* is an impressive sight. The train has a refreshment car, three first-class carriages and six second-class carriages, which together carry a full load of 500 passengers.

303

TG 2400

Chatillon
Extrémité 2

The skirt stops things from being trapped underneath the train

Bullet trains

The futuristic-looking, high-speed electric trains that run in Japan are called bullet trains. Their Japanese name is *Shinkansen*. When they were introduced in 1964, the trains provided the first passenger service in the world to travel at speeds of 161 kilometres per hour. Today, the trains reach much faster speeds of up to 300 kilometres per hour, running on specially designed tracks. Bullet trains also offer a very frequent service, and carry nearly one million passengers every day.

Speeding past Mount Fuji
This modern type of bullet train is made of aluminium alloy for lightness and speed.

The driver sits high up and has a clear view of the line ahead

High-speed journey
The Series 100 bullet train has a top speed of 228 kilometres per hour. It has cut the intercity journey time from Tokyo to Osaka, a distance of 516 kilometres, to three hours.

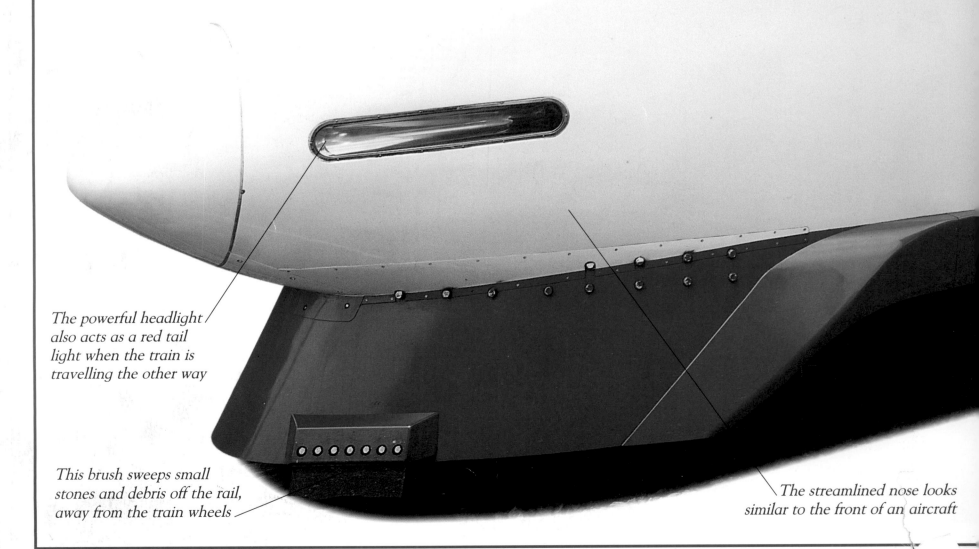

The powerful headlight also acts as a red tail light when the train is travelling the other way

This brush sweeps small stones and debris off the rail, away from the train wheels

The streamlined nose looks similar to the front of an aircraft

Train of the future

This unusual looking train, currently in development, has no wheels. It is called a maglev, which is short for "magnetic levitation". Strong magnets on the bottom of the train and on the track raise the train a few centimetres off the ground, and a powerful magnetic field moves the train along. The reduced friction means that the train can travel at amazing speeds of up to 550 kilometres per hour.

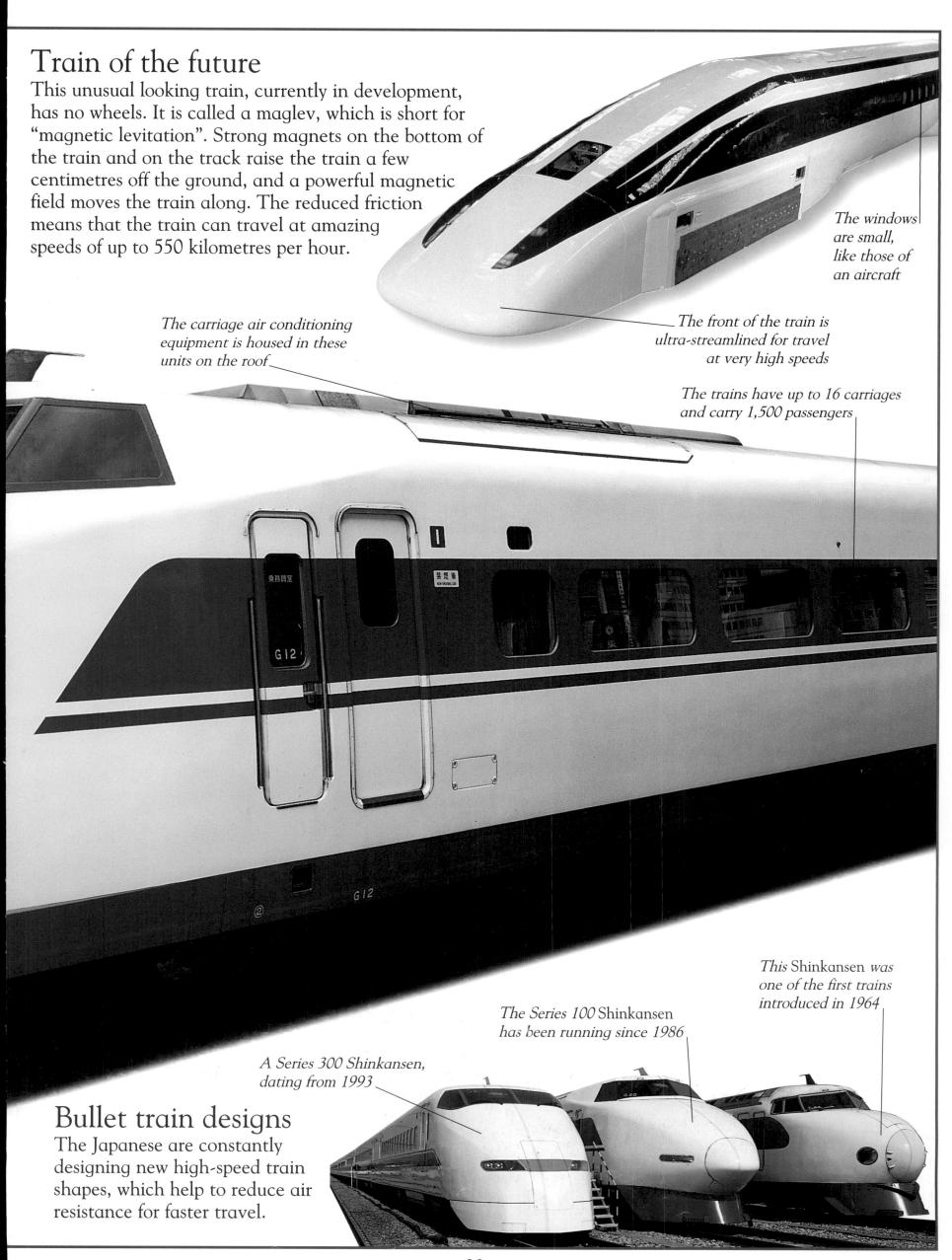

The windows are small, like those of an aircraft

The carriage air conditioning equipment is housed in these units on the roof

The front of the train is ultra-streamlined for travel at very high speeds

The trains have up to 16 carriages and carry 1,500 passengers

This Shinkansen was one of the first trains introduced in 1964

The Series 100 Shinkansen has been running since 1986

A Series 300 Shinkansen, dating from 1993

Bullet train designs

The Japanese are constantly designing new high-speed train shapes, which help to reduce air resistance for faster travel.

High-speed passenger trains

There is a driving car at both ends of the train, so that at the end of each journey, the train is immediately ready to depart

Electric trains are now running at faster and faster speeds, because they have to compete with cars and aeroplanes for passengers travelling between major cities. High-speed passenger trains run on electric power picked up from overhead lines. Some countries have built brand-new railway networks for their fast electric trains. Others run a high-speed service on existing tracks and fit the trains into their normal rail schedules.

Head or tail lights are used, depending on which way the train is travelling

Fast and slow tracks

Germany's high-speed trains run on both existing tracks and newly built lines. The ICE electric engines can only run at their top speed of 280 kilometres per hour when travelling on the new lines.

The lip on the power car acts as a small snowplough

The driving trailer has space for carrying luggage

England to Scotland

Britain's GNER 225 has a top speed of 225 kilometres per hour. It runs between London and Edinburgh on the line operated by the Great North Eastern Railway.

24

Travelling on straight lines

The new Italian ETR 500 can travel at 300 kilometres per hour. It runs on specially built high-speed routes with few curves. This means that the train can maintain its fast speed without slowing down for bends or other traffic on the line.

The pantograph picks up electric power from overhead wires

Tilting train

The railways of Sweden are all twists and turns. The engine and carriages of the X2000 train tilt when going around corners. This enables the train to keep up its top speed of 200 kilometres per hour.

The X2000 power car pulls five passenger carriages on its intercity journeys

Mountain trains

Railways are very popular in mountainous areas where it would be difficult to build a road. Many mountain railways were built just so that people could enjoy the view from the train. Rack railways have special tracks that can run up the sides of mountains. Under the engine, the train has a powered cog wheel, which grips a toothed rail. This allows the train to climb very steep slopes and prevents it from slipping backwards.

World's highest railway
The Huancayo to Huancay line in Peru is the world's highest railway. This ordinary railway reaches a height of 4,830 metres. The steam locomotives that run here were built in England.

Tourist train
The Brienz Rothorn train is now a tourist attraction. This rack railway is 7.5 kilometres long and is the only one in Switzerland that still uses steam locomotives. Powerful engines push the passenger carriages up the mountainside, to a height of 1,680 metres.

The passenger carriage is pushed uphill by the steam locomotive

A cogged wheel on the engine climbs up the toothed rack

The locomotive is built at an angle so that it stays level on the steep slope

Bridges and tunnels
Railways in mountainous areas have to use many bridges, viaducts, and tunnels to pass through difficult terrain. This train is called the *Glacier Express* because it runs through deep snow for many months of the year. It carries passengers to ski resorts in the Swiss mountains.

Steepest rack railway

The Mount Pilatus Railway in Switzerland is the steepest rack railway in the world. The railway used steam engines when it was opened in 1889, but electric trains took over in 1937. The trains are single carriages and have a top speed of nine kilometres per hour.

The pantograph collects electricity from the wires running overhead

The carriages are specially designed so that the passenger seats match the angle of the slope

Some sections of the track slide sideways to enable trains to pass each other

Trains travel up and down the mountain on the same track

The rack is laid between the ordinary rails

Hanging train

The Wuppertal monorail, in Germany, is built over a river. The hanging carriages are like an ordinary train, but the driving wheels are on the roof.

The train is powered by electric motors

Rails run in both directions

Giant, steel legs support the monorail track

The stations are at the same level as the track. Passengers reach the platforms by escalator

Monorail

These special trains hang or balance on a single rail, called a monorail. The trains have motors, which are powered by electricity. Monorail trains run high up off the ground and carry passengers across busy cities, travelling over the tops of roads, buildings, and rivers. Riding on a monorail seems like flying and can be very exciting.

Streamlined train

The Sydney Harbourlink monorail, in Australia, is streamlined. The driver's cab has a sloping windscreen, so it looks very futuristic. However, the train travels quite slowly at about 30 kilometres per hour.

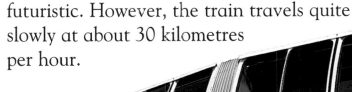

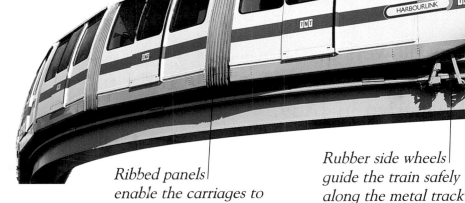

Avoiding the busy traffic

People use the Wuppertal monorail like a bus to travel to work, or to the shops. Some children even go to school on it.

Ribbed panels enable the carriages to travel round tight bends

Rubber side wheels guide the train safely along the metal track

The windscreen wiper helps the driver to have a clear view ahead

Monorails for fun

Some monorails, like the Seattle Expo Alweg, in the United States of America, are built to take visitors around a large exhibition or fun park. The cars have big windows so everyone can see out and get a good view. Monorails usually only have one or two carriages, which can carry up to 100 people.

Sliding doors let the passengers in and out at stations

The train carriages straddle the concrete track

The wheels run along the top of the rail and take the train's weight. Guide wheels run along the sides to keep the train balanced

Snow trains

When railway lines become blocked by snow, special trains are needed to dig out the tracks so that trains can start running again. Snowploughs can be used to clear deep snowdrifts, but in really severe conditions, rotary snow blowers are needed to open up the line. These snow trains were first used in the United States of America in 1869.

Loose snow was broken up by the wheel, blown out of this chute, and thrown clear of the track

The powerful headlight could light up the track in blizzard conditions

Large side blades sliced a path through the snowdrifts and channelled the snow into the spinning wheel

The giant spinning wheel broke up the snow

The snow blower was powered by steam from a boiler inside the blower

Clearing tracks

Snow blowers clear the line before other trains start running. In very heavy snow storms, they may be needed to rescue stranded trains.

Diesel power

This British snow train is diesel powered and does not need a locomotive to push it. Large blades break up the snow, which is then blown clear of the track. Deep snow is rare in Britain, so the train is stored in a depot when not in use.

Snow blower at work

This steam-powered snow blower clears the line by cutting into the snowdrift and then blowing the loose snow away from the line. The train can clear about 40 metres of deep snow per minute and is moved along the line by "pusher" locomotives.

The tender carried the coal and water to fuel the boiler

This vehicle contained equipment and facilities for the crew

White Pass

White Pass

Steam snow blower

This snow blower worked on the railroads of Alaska, in America, and was powered by steam. It had a crew of three: the fireman, the engineer who looked after the machinery, and the pilot who signalled to the "pusher" locomotives.

Glossary

Bogie
A set of four wheels fitted under a locomotive or wagon to help it turn on curved track.

Boiler
The large metal drum on a steam locomotive, where the water is turned into steam.

Car or Carriage
The coaches that carry passengers on a train.

Coke
A type of coal used as fuel for early steam locomotives.

Connecting rod
A metal rod that links the piston to the driving wheels of a steam locomotive.

Coupling
A device for joining carriages to an engine and to each other to form a train.

Coupling rod
The metal rod that links a pair of driving wheels together.

Cylinder
The metal tube in which steam or gas under pressure pushes the piston to drive the wheels.

Diesel-electric engine
A locomotive using diesel oil as the fuel to generate electricity, which in turn powers electric motors that drive the wheels.

Driving wheels
The main wheels that are connected to a power supply and move a locomotive.

Electric engine
A locomotive powered by electricity picked up from an electric cable or third rail.

Firebox
The metal box behind a steam locomotive's boiler, where the fuel is burned.

Fireman
The person on a steam engine who shovels coal into the firebox and keeps the boiler topped up with water.

Footplate
The driver's cab on a steam engine.

Locomotive
The vehicle that provides the power to move a train.

Pantograph
A metal frame on top of an electric locomotive, which picks up electricity from cables hanging above the track.

Piston rod
The moving rod inside a cylinder that helps to turn a locomotive's driving wheels.

Power car
A diesel or electric locomotive permanently joined to a set of passenger carriages.

Third rail
A rail on the ground that supplies electricity to some electric trains.

Wagon
A train vehicle that carries freight, or goods.

Index of trains

Big Boy 10
Brienz Rothorn train 26
Bullet train 22, 23

Canadian Trans-continental 14
Challenger 11

ETR 500 25
Eurostar 16, 18, 19

Flying Scotsman 9

Garratt 10, 11
Glacier Express 26
GNER 225 24

Huancayo to Huancay train 26

ICE 24

Jupiter 6

Locomotive 119 6, 7

Maglev 23
Mallard 8, 9
Mount Pilatus train 27

Puffing Billy 5

Rocket 4

Santa Fe freight train 12, 13
Seattle Expo Alweg monorail 29
Le Shuttle 16, 17, 18
Sir Nigel Gresley 8
snow blower 30, 31
Sydney Harbourlink monorail 29

TGV 18, 20, 21
Trans-Siberian Express 15

Wuppertal monorail 28, 29

X2000 24, 25